The
TREE-MENDOUS
CHRISTMAS
Activity
BOOK

BUSTER BOOKS

ILLUSTRATED BY KATHRYN SELBERT
WRITTEN AND EDITED BY ZOE CLARK
DESIGNED BY ZOE BRADLEY
COVER DESIGN BY ANGIE ALLISON

First published in Great Britain in 2023 by Buster Books, an imprint of
Michael O'Mara Books Limited, 9 Lion Yard, Tremadoc Road, London SW4 7NQ

W www.mombooks.com/buster   f Buster Books   🐦 @BusterBooks   📷 @buster_books

Copyright © Buster Books 2023

With additional material adapted from www.shutterstock.com

ISBN: 978-1-78055-918-6

1 3 5 7 9 10 8 6 4 2

This book was printed in June 2023 by Leo Paper Products Ltd,
Heshan Astros Printing Limited, Xuantan Temple Industrial Zone,
Gulao Town, Heshan City, Guangdong Province, China.

HO HO HO!

Get your puzzling hat on with this jolly collection
of fun and festive games and activities. Packed with
wintry wonders, excited elves and tasty treats, this
book is bursting with Christmas cheer.

There are merry mazes, spot-the-difference puzzles,
cute colouring challenges, search-and-find scenes,
memory games and much more. All the answers
are at the back of the book if you get stuck.

Time to dive in and get Christmas cracking!

TREE TOPPER TIDY UP

Can you untangle the Christmas lights to work out which tree topper belongs at the top of each tree?

A.

B.

C.

D.

1.

2.

3.

4.

ICE-SKATING FUN

Can you spot ten differences between the two scenes below?

HUNGRY HIKE

Help this hungry elf munch their way to a Christmas feast by following the order below. You can move across, up and down, but not diagonally.

ORDER TO FOLLOW:

Start

Finish

FESTIVE FRIENDS

Can you put these reindeer friends in order
of size from smallest to largest? Write
the correct order in the spaces below.

....

WINTRY WORKSHOP

These elves are busy wrapping presents in Santa's workshop.
Count how many items in the checklist you can spot hidden
in the picture. Do your totals match the ones shown?

CHECKLIST:

4 3 6 2 2

CANDY CANE CLUTTER

How many candy canes can you count in this jumble?

SNAZZY STOCKINGS

Each Christmas stocking has a pattern on it that matches a pattern on one of the presents below. Look closely at the pictures and match each stocking with the correct gift.

ROUNDABOUT REINDEER

Help this little reindeer through the maze to the finish
line. How many carrots do you pick up on the way?
Make sure you avoid the icy pond and trees!

Start

Finish

GINGERBREAD GENIUS

Study this gingerbread house for two minutes.
Then turn the page and see how much
you can remember about it.

GINGERBREAD GENIUS (CONTINUED)

Once you've looked at the picture on the previous page, see if you can answer these questions without turning back.

1. How many windows does the house have?

....

2. How many lollipop trees are there in the garden?

....

3. True or false? The house has a chimney.

....

4. How many yellow sweets are on the roof of the house?

....

5. True or false? There are three sweetie stepping stones.

....

6. What colour is the front door?

....

HOT CHOC TOPPINGS

Add your favourite toppings to this warming mug of hot chocolate, then decorate it and colour it in!

PRESENT PILE
Which group contains all the items shown at the top of the page?

DECK THE HALLS

Which shadow matches this
festive wreath exactly?

A.

B.

C.

D.

E.

DANCING DELIGHT

Look at this colourful Christmas scene. Can you
work out which three close-ups at the bottom
of the page do not appear in the main picture?

A.   B.   C.   D.   E.   F.

CHRISTMAS COOKIES

Look closely at the seasonal sequences of sweet treats below. Can you fill in the missing items to complete the patterns?

WINTER WOODLAND

Can you spot ten differences between the
two pictures of these festive friends?

SWEET TREATS

Can you find the following groups of
Christmas treats in the grid below?

A.

B.

C.

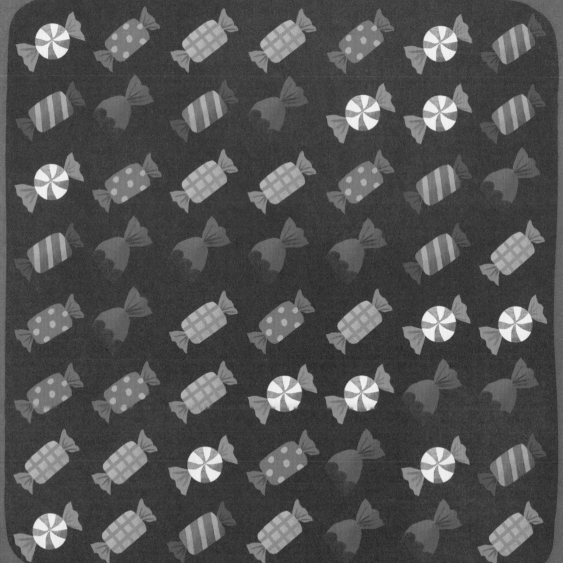

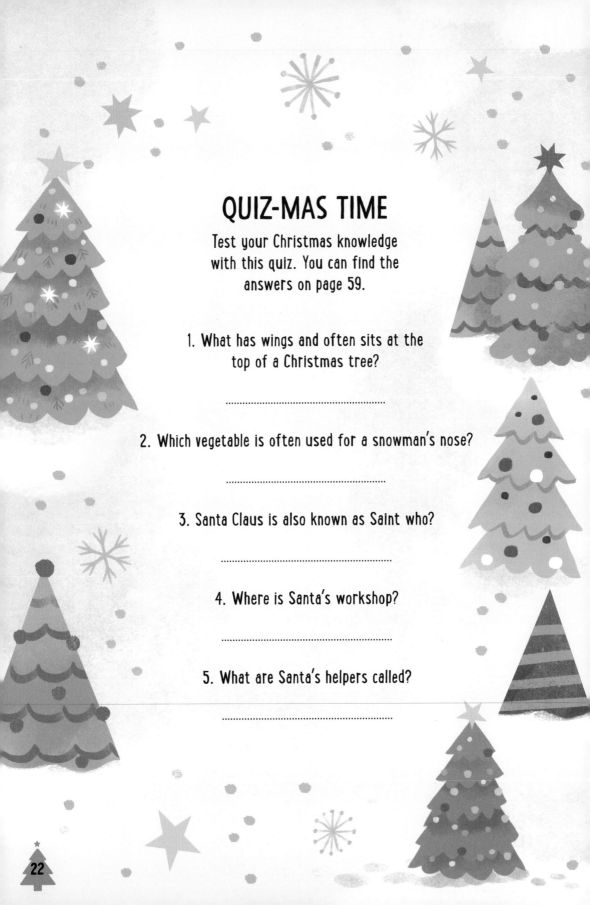

QUIZ-MAS TIME

Test your Christmas knowledge
with this quiz. You can find the
answers on page 59.

1. What has wings and often sits at the
top of a Christmas tree?

....

2. Which vegetable is often used for a snowman's nose?

....

3. Santa Claus is also known as Saint who?

....

4. Where is Santa's workshop?

....

5. What are Santa's helpers called?

....

JOLLY JUMPER

Decorate and colour in your very own
Christmas jumper in any way you like.

MERRY MOUNTAIN

Which elf is sledging down the path that leads
to Santa's grotto? Guide Santa's little helpers
down the snowy mountain to find out.

A.

B.

SANTA'S
GROTTO

ODD SNOWMAN OUT

Can you spot the snowman that is different to the others? Then count how many snowmen there are and write your total in the space below.

TOTAL: ....

CHRISTMAS COTTAGE

Can you work out which of the four
jigsaw pieces is from the picture?

A.

B.

C.

D.

CHRISTMAS WISHES

These Christmas cards have been left unfinished.
Decorate and colour them in, then fill in your
Christmas wish list.

Dear Santa

_____

_____

_____

_____

_____

_____

_____

_____

_____

TOPPLING TOWERS

Can you fill in the missing numbers in each sequence on these Christmas present towers? Start at the bottom and work your way up.

Tower 1 (top to bottom): 25, 50, ___, 100, 125, ___, 175

Tower 2 (top to bottom): 18, 16, 14, ___, 10, 8, 6, ___

Tower 3 (top to bottom): 7, ___, 19, 25, 31, ___, 43

SNOWBALL FIGHT

These elves are having fun in the snow. Can you untangle the lines to work out which elf threw which snowball? Which elf threw the snowball that didn't hit anyone?

MISCHIEVOUS MIX-UP

These mischievous elves have muddled up their hats!
Can you use the clues to work out which hat belongs
to which elf? Write the correct name under each hat.

COOKIE
My hat has green
fur around the bottom.

FIGGY
My hat is covered
in stars.

SUGARPLUM
My hat has five
bows on it.

BUDDY
My hat has a bell on the end.

PIXIE
My hat has tasty treats on it.

CHRISTMAS CUPCAKES

These cupcakes are just waiting to be eaten.
Can you match up the five identical pairs?
Circle the cupcake that is not one of a pair.

SNOWY SPOT-THE-DIFFERENCE

Can you spot ten differences
between the two pictures?

JOLLY JUMBLE

How many Christmas stockings
can you count in this jumble?

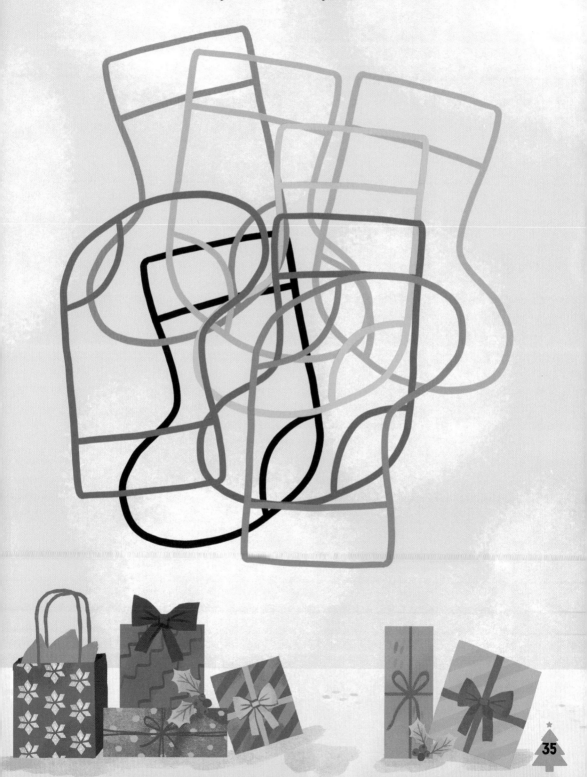

SNOW-DOKU

Can you complete this sudoku challenge? There should be one gingerbread man, one snowflake, one present and one Santa hat in each row, column and four-square box.

MERRY MAIL

Can you help deliver these letters to Santa?
You can only land on numbers that are in the
three times table and next to each other.

Start

3   5   15

6   13   8

7   9   10

12   11

19

15   18   17   23

10   21   20

19   22   24   25

27

31   28   30

29   32   33

Finish

CHRISTMAS CAROL

Can you find seven musical instruments
among these Christmas carolling friends?

HOLIDAY HOLLY

All of these pieces of holly look the same,
apart from one — can you spot it?

TREMENDOUS TREE

Count how many items in the checklist you can spot in the scene below. Do your totals match the ones shown?

CHECKLIST: 8

5   6

3   2

COSY CORNER

Which two tiles cannot be found in this festive scene?
Can you spot four presents hidden in the main picture, too?

A.

B.

C.

D.

E.

LAKESIDE LEAPING

Can you help this reindeer leap across the frozen lake to join their family? You can only jump on the patches of ice that have five sides and are next to each other.

Start

Finish

43

PRETTY PAIRS

Can you match up the pairs of snowflakes
that look the same? Circle the snowflake
that is not one of a pair.

WINDOW SHOPPING

Study this Christmas window display for two minutes.
Try to remember as much of the scene as possible,
then turn the page and test your memory.

WINDOW SHOPPING (CONTINUED)

Once you've looked at the picture on the previous page, see
if you can answer these questions without turning back.

1. How many presents are there in the picture?

....

2. Does the Christmas wreath have a yellow star or a red bow on it?

....

3. What colour are the curtains at the top of the window?

....

4. True or false? There are two snowglobes in the picture.

....

5. Is the rabbit at the bottom of the picture green or pink?

....

6. True or false? The rocking horse has a gingerbread man on it.

....

SNOW DOGS

Which shadow matches this
Christmassy canine exactly?

FESTIVE FIX-UP

Oh no, Santa's sleigh is broken! Can you work out
which five pieces below fit together to repair it?

DOTTY DECORATIONS

Join the dots to complete this lovely Christmas stocking. When you're finished, colour it in!

CHRISTMAS COUNTERS

Challenge your friends and family to this Christmas counter game.
You'll need a counter for each player and one dice. Take turns to roll the dice
and move your counter along the snowy path. It's a race to the finish line!

START

You build an awesome gingerbread house. **Move forwards one space.**

Everyone loves your yummy Christmas cookies. **Move forwards two spaces.**

Your Christmas wish list arrives with Santa. **Move forwards one space.**

Your delicious Christmas dinner is ready. **Move forwards to the finish line.**

FINISH

You are finished
wrapping all
your presents.
**Move forwards
two spaces.**

Your snowman
is melting!
**Move back
one space.**

You sled down
a super-fun hill.
**Move forwards
two spaces.**

Your Christmas cards
get lost in the post.
Move back two spaces.

ELF EXCITEMENT

It's almost Christmas! Can you match each
of these excited elves with their shadows?

SLEIGH BELLS

It's Christmas Eve and Santa is on his way! Which chimney is he heading to first? Follow the coordinates to help guide Santa's sleigh to his first stop, then write the correct coordinate in the space below.

1. Start at A1
2. Move 4 squares UP to A5
3. Move 5 squares RIGHT to F5
4. Move 3 squares DOWN to F2
5. Move 3 squares LEFT to C2
6. Move 1 square UP to ...

In which coordinate is the chimney Santa is heading to first? ....

FATHER CHRISTMAS

Can you find the Santa Claus that matches the clues below?

1. I am wearing black gloves.
2. I have a sack full of presents.
3. My hat is green.

C.

E.

D.

55

ANSWERS

PAGE 4: TREE TOPPER TIDY UP

A = 2   C = 1
B = 4   D = 3

PAGE 5: ICE-SKATING FUN

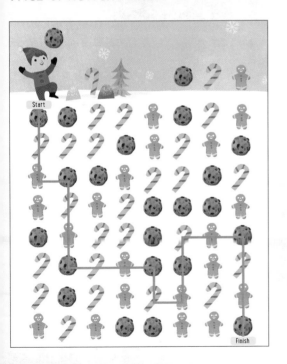

PAGES 8-9: WINTRY WORKSHOP

PAGE 10: CANDY CANE CLUTTER

Answer: 11

PAGE 6: HUNGRY HIKE

PAGE 11: SNAZZY STOCKINGS

PAGE 7: FESTIVE FRIENDS

B, F, E, C, A, D

A = 3   C = 2
B = 4   D = 1

PAGE 12: ROUNDABOUT REINDEER

There are four carrots on the correct path.

PAGES 13–14: GINGERBREAD GENIUS

1. The house has four windows.
2. There are three lollipop trees in the garden.
3. True, the house has a chimney.
4. There are eight yellow sweets on the roof of the house.
5. False, there are five sweetie stepping stones.
6. The front door is pink.

PAGE 16: PRESENT PILE

Answer: C

PAGE 17: DECK THE HALLS

Answer: E

PAGE 18: DANCING DELIGHT

Answers: A, D and F

PAGE 19: CHRISTMAS COOKIES

58

PAGE 20: WINTER WOODLAND

PAGE 21: SWEET TREATS

PAGE 22: QUIZ-MAS TIME

Answers:
1. An angel
2. A carrot
3. Saint Nicholas
4. The North Pole
5. Elves

PAGES 24-25: MERRY MOUNTAIN

Answer: B

PAGE 26: ODD SNOWMAN OUT

There are 11 snowmen in total.

PAGE 27: CHRISTMAS COTTAGE

Answer: B

PAGE 30: TOPPLING TOWERS

PAGE 31: SNOWBALL FIGHT

A = 5
B = 2
C = 4
D = 1
E = 3

Elf E threw the snowball that didn't hit anyone.

PAGE 32: MISCHIEVOUS MIX-UP

1. Buddy
2. Cookie
3. Sugarplum
4. Figgy
5. Pixie

PAGE 33: CHRISTMAS CUPCAKES

PAGE 36: SNOW-DOKU

PAGE 34: SNOWY SPOT-THE-DIFFERENCE

PAGE 37: MERRY MAIL

PAGE 35: JOLLY JUMBLE
Answer: 8

PAGE 38: CHRISTMAS CAROL

PAGE 40: TREMENDOUS TREE

PAGE 39: HOLIDAY HOLLY

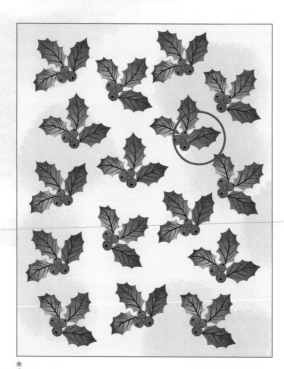

PAGE 41: COSY CORNER

Answers: A and E

PAGES 42–43: LAKESIDE LEAPING

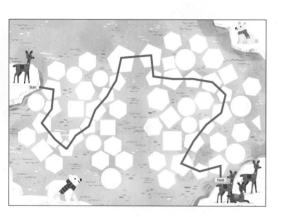

PAGE 44: PRETTY PAIRS

PAGES 45–46: WINDOW SHOPPING

1. There are eight presents in the picture.
2. The wreath has a red bow on it.
3. The curtains are blue.
4. True, there are two snowglobes.
5. The rabbit is pink.
6. False, it is a nutcracker.

PAGE 47: SNOW DOGS

Answer: D

PAGE 48: FESTIVE FIX-UP

PAGE 49: DOTTY DECORATIONS

PAGE 52: ELF EXCITEMENT

A = 2   C = 3
B = 4   D = 1

PAGE 53: SLEIGH BELLS

Santa is heading to coordinate C3 first.

PAGES 54-55: FATHER CHRISTMAS

Answer: C